# KEEPING ISRAEL SAFE

## Serving in the
## Israel Defense Forces

# KEEPING ISRAEL SAFE

## Serving in the Israel Defense Forces

Barbara Sofer

KAR-BEN
PUBLISHING

KAR-BEN PUBLISHING
A division of Lerner Publishing Group, Inc.
241 First Avenue North
Minneapolis, MN 55401 U.S.A.
1-800-4KARBEN

Website address: www.karben.com

Library of Congress Cataloging-in-Publication Data

Sofer, Barbara.
    Keeping Israel Safe : The Israel Defense Forces / by Barbara Sofer.
        p. cm.
    Includes bibliographical references.
    ISBN 978-0-8225-7221-3 (lib. bdg. : alk. paper) 1. Israel. Tseva haganah le-Yisra'el.
  2. Israel—Armed forces—Juvenile literature.  I. Title.
  UA853.I8S59  2008
  355.0095694—dc22                                           2006100175

Manufactured in the United States of America
1 2 3 4 5 6 — JR – 12 11 10 09 08 07

# CONTENTS

# CHAPTER 1
# "We're Going to the Army"

"**P**lease pass the ketchup, David," Sharona said, reaching across the table. "You don't have to finish the whole bottle."

David, a redhead like the biblical King David, smiled and held the squeeze bottle up to the light to show it was still half full. "Don't exaggerate. There's plenty left." The others laughed.

Dana, David, Sharona, and Hezzy were sitting at a booth in a fast-food restaurant next door to the Jerusalem municipal swimming pool. David's love of ketchup was an old joke among them.

It was the last day of summer vacation. Getting together before the start of school had been their tradition since first grade. They'd all met when Sharona's older sister Miri had organized a day camp for the four of them in the shelter of the new apartment building they'd all moved into that summer. Hezzy and Sharona had always lived in Jerusalem. David's family had moved there from Haifa, and Dana's family had recently emigrated from the United States, so they were particularly happy to meet the other children in the building.

On the last day of camp, Miri had taken them out for burgers, and they continued the tradition each year. Growing up in the same apartment building, the four of them had remained close, even though they went to different schools.

Dana lifted up her soda to make a toast. "Here's to Miri and her day camp. She seemed so grown up back then, but she was only 18, a year older than we are. It was the summer right before she went into the army."

The four teens were starting their senior year and would be going into the army after graduation, the boys for at least three years, the girls for at least two. They'd already received call-up notices and had gone for interviews and tests at the Induction Center.

"When we were in Miri's camp, we liked to play soldiers," David said. "Now it's for real. By next summer, we'll all be soldiers. I brought a camera. Let's ask someone to take our picture." A woman in the next booth offered. The friends put their arms around one another's shoulders. "Smile," said Dana.

"Speaking of photos, Hezzy, remember the picture you showed us of your great-grandfather Alexander on

A member of Hashomer, a pre-military guard group established by early Jewish settlers.

horseback, carrying a gun. He was a *Shomer* guard. That was before Israel was even a state."

"I have photos of my grandfather in uniform too," said Sharona. "He was our age – not even 18 — when he fought in the War of Independence."

"I don't understand," said Dana. "How could he be in the army when he was so young?"

"Back then, there weren't enough soldiers. Many teenagers were so eager to join the army they pretended to be older than they really were," David said. "You could never do that today. You have to submit school records, take tests, and go for personal interviews."

"My grandparents came to Israel as immigrants after World War II, and my grandfather went straight into the army as soon as he got off the boat," Sharona told the group. "He didn't even speak Hebrew very well."

Dana sighed. "I always feel funny when you talk about

your sisters, brothers, parents, and grandparents in the army. I'll be the first soldier in my family. What if my parents don't know they're supposed to send me packages of cookies?"

"Are you kidding?" Sharona laughed. "In an apartment building like ours, with all four of us in the army, our parents will be talking about us all the time."

"And don't think that because we've all had so many relatives in the army that we're not a little scared," said Hezzy, blushing. "Even me."

"Besides, it's not like the old days," said Sharona. "We'll all have cell phones; we'll be able to talk to each other, and we'll see each other on leave."

She was quiet for a moment. "But it does seem strange that we'll be the army and have to follow orders. That's the part that worries me. You know me—I argue a lot with my parents and even with my teachers. I'm sort of bossy. It's easier for me to give orders than to take orders." Then she smiled. "Let's order dessert!"

Young teens often pretended to be older
so they could join the Haganah.

## BACK TO THE BIBLE

Israeli soldiers see themselves as the continuation of a military tradition
that stretches back to the time of the Bible. Heroes such as Joshua,
Samson, King David, and Deborah still serve as inspiration thousands of
years later.

But the current Israeli army has more recent origins. When the
Jews began returning to their homeland in the 19th century, the whole
area was called Palestine and had been ruled by Turkey since the
16th century.

The early Jewish settlers had to organize guards to protect
themselves against marauding Arabs. The best known of these pre-
military guard groups was *Hashomer*, founded in 1909. More than one
hundred men and women belonged. The work was dangerous. The guards
received payment from the towns and settlements they protected.

# BRITISH RULE

At the end of World War I (1914–1918), the British defeated the Turkish army and conquered territory that included Palestine. During the war, Jewish soldiers had fought in a British army unit called *Hagedud Ha-ivri* (the Jewish Legion). David Ben-Gurion, who would become Israel's first prime minister, volunteered for the Jewish Legion.

In 1917 the British set up a protectorate government in Palestine. At first, the members of Hashomer thought there would no longer be a need for their services, but they were wrong. The British did not protect them. In 1920 Arabs attacked Jewish settlements in the Galilee and riots broke out in Jerusalem. To face the worsening attacks, Hashomer was replaced by a much larger organization called the *Haganah*, which is Hebrew for "defense."

Women members of Haganah undergo training.

In pre-state Israel, arms were manufactured and stored in secret.

## THE HAGANAH

The Haganah was made up of men and women who had volunteered for Hashomer, along with soldiers who had fought in The Jewish Legion. Most of the Haganah had no fighting experience. To prepare future soldiers, a youth unit, the *Gadna*, was created to provide military training for 14- to 18-year-olds. Younger teens often pretended to be older so they could join. The Haganah had to work in secret because the British rulers didn't want an underground army in the area. Members of the Haganah would be arrested if caught. Arms had to be manufactured secretly and were stored in secret hiding places called *slikim*.

The strength and skill of the Haganah was tested in 1929, when Arab rioters attacked the Jewish communities of Jerusalem, Tel Aviv, and Haifa.

## PALMACH

The Palmach (short for *plugot mahatz* – strike force) was a special unit of the Haganah. Its members supported themselves by living and working on communal farms called kibbutzim. When not training, they plowed fields and picked fruit. They had a strong feeling of comradeship among them and spent their evenings sitting around campfires, exchanging stories.

When World War II (1939–1945) broke out, some Palmach soldiers volunteered for commando assignments in the British army and received special training. They were famous for quick and daring strikes against the Nazis. Yitzhak Rabin, who would become Prime Minister of Israel, was in the Palmach.

Because the British were unwilling to allow Jews trying to escape from war-torn Europe to enter Palestine, members of the Haganah helped organize a system to smuggle refugees into the country. These soldiers,

The Haganah helped smuggle illegal immigrants from ship to shore.

called *palyam*, went out into the water at night and carried the illegal immigrants from ships to the shore.

In 1944 two additional underground organizations, *Etzel* (also called the *Irgun*) and *Lehi*, were formed. They began attacking British institutions to try to convince them to leave Palestine. Yitzhak Shamir and Menachem Begin, two leaders of these groups, would one day become Prime Ministers of the State of Israel.

Israel defense soldier guards the police station at Kibbutz Gesher during the War of Independence.

During The War of Independence, Israel had few tanks and used trucks and buses reinforced with iron plates.

Later, the Haganah also decided to join the fight against the British, forming a united resistance to help the country gain its independence. On June 17, 1946, in an action called Night of the Bridges, eleven bridges linking Palestine to the neighboring countries were blown up. By morning, the country was safely cut off from its surrounding enemies.

## WAR OF INDEPENDENCE

On November 29, 1947, the United Nations voted for a Partition Plan to divide Palestine, giving part to the Jews and part to the Arabs. The Jews accepted this plan, but the Arabs didn't. Nevertheless, the British government announced that it would withdraw from the area on May 15, 1948. Even before that date, battles were waged between the Arabs and the Jews. In April, a month before the British left Palestine, Arabs attacked a convoy of ambulances and buses traveling to Hadassah Hospital on Jerusalem's Mount Scopus, killing 78 doctors, nurses, patients, and students.

On May 14, 1948, a day before the scheduled British withdrawal, an independent State of Israel was declared by David Ben-Gurion, who became its first Prime Minister. That very night, Egyptian planes attacked

Some Bedouin and Druze soldiers served alongside Israelis in The War of Independence.

Tel Aviv. The armies of all the neighboring Arab countries surrounded the new state, attacking towns, villages, and kibbutzim.

Israel didn't yet have an army or an air force; there were only the underground fighters. Eleven days into independence, the new government decided to turn the Haganah and other forces into the official army of the new state. Experienced pilots and sailors from outside Israel volunteered for the new army, to help the new state defend itself.

To honor the work of the Haganah, this new army was called *TZ'va HaHaganah L'Yisrael*. The Hebrew acronym is *TZaHaL*. In English it is called the Israel Defense Forces, or IDF. Though the IDF didn't have a single tank, fighter plane, or field gun, it was facing experienced armies. The Syrians invaded from the north, the Egyptians from the south, and the Jordanians and Iraqis from the east. On the west was the Mediterranean Sea, but Arab governments broadcast over and over that their goal was to "throw the Jews into the sea."

The very tough fight for independence lasted until March 1949. In the process, 6,000 men and women — soldiers and civilians — were killed.

# A YOUNG ARMY IN A YOUNG COUNTRY

To meet the needs of wartime, the IDF had been established quickly. When the war was over, officers finally had time to think about how they wanted to build their army. Generals traveled to countries around the world to study how other armies were organized.

They decided that both men and women would be drafted at the age of 18. After mandatory service, they would continue to serve in reserve units, called *milu'im*, which could be called up to support the regular army in times of trouble. At a moment's notice, doctors, mechanics, or university professors could be asked to leave their jobs and report for active duty. Women would remain in the reserves until the age of 24, but men would be required to stay until the age of 54. Conceivably, a soldier might serve together with his or her father! The IDF also created its own Reserve Medical Corps of doctors and dentists who could be called up to treat sick and injured soldiers.

Israel's soldiers would do more than fight. As the population doubled following independence, they were assigned to help new immigrants learn to read, write, and speak Hebrew, and adjust to life in their new country.

## STRUCTURE OF THE IDF

### CHAIN OF COMMAND

Prime Minister

Minister of Defense

Commander of the General Staff, (Ramat Kal)

Commander of the Land, Air and Space Forces

Commander of Northern, Central, Southern
and Homeland Commands

Commander of Intelligence Forces

Commander of Logistics

All food in the IDF is kosher and there is special holiday food such as matzah.

Following Jewish tradition, all food in the IDF would be kosher and there would be special holiday food, such as matzah, for Passover.

Because they might be called upon to fight their own family members from neighboring countries, Israeli Arabs were exempt from the army. However, they could volunteer, and certain Arab groups—Druze, Circassians, and some Bedouins— serve alongside Jewish soldiers in the IDF.

Israel is a small country, so there are soldiers in almost every family. On weekends it is a familiar sight to see soldiers at bus stations coming home on leave.

## THE IDF TODAY

Today, Israel's army is one of the best in the world. There is a standing army of more than 200,000 troops, along with nearly 550,000 reservists, who can be mobilized within 24 hours in a national emergency. The IDF is known for the advanced weapons technology and sophisticated electronic systems it has developed for intelligence and communications. Many of these systems are marketed to other countries.

In 1963, the Palestine Liberation Organization, under the leadership of Yassir Arafat, embarked on a campaign of terrorism to weaken Israel. Periods of terror, called *intifada* (the Arab word for "shaking off"), still erupt. The IDF plays a major role in defending the country against terrorism.

IDF Air Force pilots celebrating their graduation.

## CHAPTER 2

# Hezzy Wants to Be a Pilot

**Hezzy had always loved airplanes.**
The shelves in his room were filled with dozens of model planes he had built. His dream was to join the air force and to become a jet or helicopter pilot. But Hezzy worried that he wouldn't make it. Just being accepted into pilot training was hard. Graduating from the course was even harder. Lots of teens wanted to be Israeli pilots, considered among the world's best. In his high school class alone, he knew at least eight kids who planned to try out for the course.

Hezzy went to a high school that emphasized science and technology. He made good grades and was a leader in the Israeli scouts. His first appointment with the army included a physical exam and two hours of written tests. Afterward, he was asked to take additional technical tests. The doctor said he was in good shape: he got a 97 profile, the highest possible, on his check-up. But no one told him how he'd done on the other tests, which included putting puzzles together quickly and answering reading comprehension questions. He was also interviewed by a psychologist to see if he had the right personality to be a pilot.

Every day Hezzy hurried home from school to check the mailbox. He knew that you needed an invitation to try out for the pilot's course. At last, he saw the brown envelope with his name on it. His heart pumped as he tore it open.

Try-outs for pilot school include a rigorous 10-day training camp.

"Yes!" he shouted, leaping in the air. He hurried to tell his parents and call his friends.

The letter invited him to take part in the next stage: a 10-day training camp where he'd have to prove his ability in marching, weapons instruction, and physical training. It would be tough. He'd also have to win the approval of the other applicants and demonstrate that he was a good leader. He knew that most of the group wouldn't pass the course, but he hoped he'd be one of the lucky ones.

Israel fought the War of Independence with borrowed planes.

## ISRAEL GETS AN AIR FORCE

As Israel's independence approached in 1948, leaders sent out word that aircraft and pilots would be needed for the new air force. Pilots from abroad, both Jewish and non-Jewish, volunteered. But the first planes that Israel could acquire were a Czech version of the Messerschmitt Bf 109G-14, built for the Germans during World War II. None of the pilots — either the Israelis or the volunteers — had ever flown a Nazi-designed plane. Nonetheless, at the time, they were the only planes Israel could get, and even these had to be bought secretly, taken apart, transported to Israel, and reassembled.

On May 29, 1948, when more than 500 Egyptian tanks began moving in a column to crush the city of Tel Aviv, the air force conducted its first major mission with its new planes and four volunteer air force pilots. No one knew that Israel had planes, so the Egyptian tank forces were surprised, and they scattered in confusion.

A few days later, sirens rang announcing still another Egyptian air attack. Egyptian planes had been bombing Tel Aviv routinely, because until then, there were no Israeli planes to challenge them. But this time, Israeli planes took to the sky. Two Egyptian Dakotas were downed, and the battle for Israel's airspace had begun.

Additional planes were needed. Israel bought Spitfires, Mustangs, and even B-17 bombers. In the War of Independence, battles were fought in Cairo and over the Negev desert. Israel's new air force owned 15 Egyptian and two Syrian planes. Israel lost 31 fliers. By the end of the war, Israel's skies were safe. Over the years, Israel's air force grew and became an essential arm of the country's defense.

## MILITARY RANKS

*Turai*-Private
*Turai-Rishon (TaRash)*—Private 1st class
*Rav-Turai (RabaT)* – Corporal
*Samal*—Sergeant
*Samal–Rishon (Sam'aR)*—Staff Sergeant
*Rav-Samal (RaS)* -Company Sergeant
*Rav-Samal Rishon (RaSar)* – Major
*Segen-Mishne (SeguM)*—Second Lieutenant
*Segen*—Lieutenant
*Seren*—Captain
*Rav-Seren*—Major
*Segun-Aluf*—Lieutenant Colonel
*Aluf Mishe*—Colonel
*Tat-Aluf*—Brigadier-General
*Aluf*—Major General
*Rav Aluf*—Lieutenant General

Soldiers at the Western Wall after liberating the Old City of Jerusalem in the Six-Day War.

## THE SIX-DAY WAR

By 1967, the hostility of Israel's Arab neighbors had grown. From the Golan Heights, the Syrians were shelling kibbutzim in the north and threatening Israel's water supply. Meanwhile, the Egyptian army was massing on Israel's southern border. On May 22, Egypt blockaded the Straits of Tiran, cutting off Israel's only shipping route.

At 7:14 on the morning of June 5, 1967, nearly the entire air force took off for neighboring countries. Only 12 Mirage jets stayed behind to defend the skies of Israel. The planes of the Egyptian, Jordanian, Syrian, and Iraqi air forces were not housed inside hangars and were, therefore, easy targets for the Israeli bombs. By the end of the first day of fighting, most of the planes of the Egyptian and Jordanian air forces and half of the Syrian air force planes had been destroyed. With the ground forces safe from air strikes, Israel was able to conquer the Sinai Peninsula and reunite Jerusalem. It took only a matter of days to be victorious in what is called the Six-Day War.

## ENTEBBE

On June 27, 1976, in Athens, Greece, four armed terrorists hijacked an Air France Airbus en route from Israel and forced it to fly to Uganda. The terrorists freed the crew and non-Jewish passengers but threatened to begin killing Israeli and Jewish passengers if hijacker demands weren't met in 48 hours. Israel stalled for time as it organized a daring rescue mission. Fortunately, the Ugandan airport had been built by an Israeli company, so the IDF could carefully plan its approach.

On July 4, Israeli soldiers boarded four Hercules transport planes and quietly made their way through stormy skies to Uganda. Two Boeing 707 jets came too, one as a forward command post and

Officer clears the way for rescued Air France hostages returning from their Entebbe ordeal.

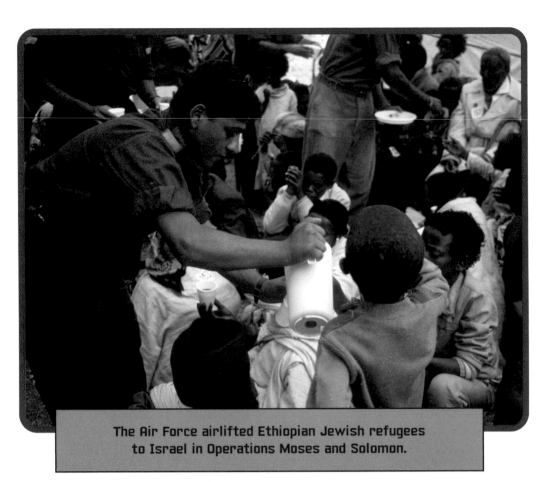

The Air Force airlifted Ethiopian Jewish refugees
to Israel in Operations Moses and Solomon.

the other as an airborne hospital. The flight took seven hours and
forty minutes. When the planes landed at 11 P.M., no one saw them
in the dark.

Col. Yonatan (Yoni) Netanyahu led the rescue force with soldiers
from a special unit of the army called *Sayeret Matkal*. He flew in
the first Hercules, which carried jeeps and a black Mercedes that
looked like the one used by Uganda's dictator Idi Amin. One of the
soldiers pretended to be the hostile dictator. In less than an hour,
the Israelis had killed the terrorists and freed the hostages.
Tragically, two hostages and Yoni Netanyahu were killed.

The date of Operation Entebbe — July 4, 1976— is easy to
remember. The United States was celebrating its bicentennial, its
200th anniversary of Independence.

## OPERATIONS MOSES AND SOLOMON

During eight months in 1984, 8,000 Ethiopian Jewish refuges were secretly flown to Israel. A year later, six Hercules transport planes brought thousands more immigrants to Israel in what was named Operation Moses. Six years later, on May 23, 1991, IDF Air Force aircraft airlifted another 14,000 Jews from Ethiopia in Operation Solomon.

In addition to caring for wounded soldiers, the IDF's medical corps has been called upon to provide humanitarian assistance to refugees and to respond to terrorist bombings and natural disasters all over the world.

## RESCUE FROM KENYA

On Hanukkah in November 2002, the Israeli Air Force rescued Israeli families vacationing in Kenya, when their holiday village was attacked by terrorists. Two Hercules transport planes were dispatched to bring doctors and medical supplies to the victims, and when a missile threatened their rescue plane, air force fighter jets flew to Kenya to escort them home.

Each plane bore the blue insignia of the Israeli Air Force. Inside the planes, the families felt safe. The IDF had come to take them home.

# CHAPTER 3
# David's Navy Hopes

**David spent the first five** years of his life in Haifa, a city on Israel's coast, and that's where he learned to swim. He was a star on the Jerusalem youth swimming team. David had always thought about joining the navy and serving as a frogman in a special underwater commando unit. There was a tough tryout for this challenging unit that included running with heavy gear on wet sand, but David felt confident. He was in good shape from all the swimming practice, and he worked out in a gym four times a week.

But two weeks before the tryouts, David was riding home from practice on the back of his cousin's motorbike. They both wore helmets, and his cousin drove carefully, but suddenly the bike hit an oil spill and turned over. David dislocated his shoulder and fractured his wrist. Worse than the pain was David's disappointment. He knew that his dream of being a frogman was over. He wouldn't be accepted into a unit that required extensive swimming or lifting. He could still serve in the army, but only in a noncombat unit.

David thought about his options. When, three weeks later, he received a letter asking him if he was interested in the Intelligence Corps, David was intrigued.

The intelligence branch of the Israeli army gathers and processes thousands of pieces of information. This is vital work, even though it means less time in the field and more time in military offices, some of them hidden in giant underground bunkers.

A lot of the information that needs to be gathered is in Arabic. David had received high marks in Arabic, so when he went for his interviews and tests, he sensed that the officers were enthusiastic about his potential.

David was accepted to the Intelligence Corps. Because intelligence work is classified, he knew he would never be able to fully share his army experience with Hezzy, Dana, and Sharona.

Sailors celebrate their induction into the Navy.

Sailors scrub their ship to make it kosher for Passover.

## ISRAEL'S NAVY

Two months before Israel became a nation, the Haganah decided to create a navy. This was a great challenge, because the sea forces of the surrounding nations were large and well established. Nonetheless, in the War of Independence, Israeli sailors managed to sink the *Emir Farouk*, the best-known ship of the Egyptian fleet.

With statehood, the Israeli Navy bought ships and equipment and began training Israeli sailors, so that it has become an important branch of the IDF. Israel's navy fights military battles, but it also functions as a coast guard.

During the Yom Kippur War in 1973, navy forces intercepted and sank four Egyptian missile boats. At the entrance to the Syrian port of Latakia, naval forces fought the first sea-to-sea missile battle in the history of naval warfare.

Today, Israeli sailors intercept boats that are unsafe, as well as boats carrying illegal goods or harboring terrorists. The Israeli Navy operates in the ports of Haifa and Ashdod along Israel's Mediterranean seacoast and in the southern

Field agents relay intelligence information.

port of Eilat on the Red Sea. The navy maintains fast attack craft, missile boats, submarines, maritime reconnaissance aircraft, and rescue helicopters.

## NAVAL COMMANDOS

Underwater commandos, who are trained for water-based and sabotage operations, take a 20-month course of intensive combat training as well as naval surface and underwater instruction. They are taught to destroy enemy craft and to undertake complicated ground operations.

## THE KARINE A

On January 2, 2002, Israeli navy commandos seized the *Karine A*, a ship trying to smuggle massive quantities of weapons, mostly from Iran, into Gaza. The ship was owned by the Palestinian Authority and captained by

Israel Intelligence is composed of soldiers and civilians
who prepare Israel to fight terrorists.

a member of the Palestinian Security Force. During the last week of
December, naval commandos set off for the Red Sea from Eilat. On the day
of the capture, Israeli planes and helicopters joined the coordinated effort,
forcing the crew to surrender.

## ISRAELI INTELLIGENCE

Soldiers who serve in the Intelligence branch play an important role
preparing Israel to face enemy threats. They analyze information from
field agents and read satellite pictures.

Israeli Intelligence is composed of both soldiers and civilians. In the
army, there's a head of military intelligence, called *Rosh Aman*, and a
military intelligence corps called *Aman*. Another section of Israeli
Intelligence is the General Security Services (GSS), referred to by the
nicknames *SHaBak* or *Shin Bet*. These agents gather information about
possible terrorist threats inside of Israel and the adjacent territories.
The GSS reports to the Prime Minister. Its activities are classified.

The Institute for Intelligence and Special Operations, better known as the *Mossad* is the branch that sends agents outside of the country to protect Israelis and Jews in communities around the world. Like the GSS, these operatives can be either soldiers or civilians. The Mossad reports to the Prime Minister's office. Even though the GSS and the Mossad aren't IDF units and operatives don't wear uniforms, working in these security units counts as military service.

One of the Mossad's famous actions resulted in the capture of Nazi mass murderer Adolf Eichmann in Argentina. Another was sending Israeli agent Eli Cohen to Syria. The information he provided was essential for winning the Six-Day War. Tragically, Cohen was captured and killed.

After terrorists murdered eleven Israeli athletes at the Olympic Games in Munich in 1972, the Mossad tracked down the Black September terrorists connected to the murders. The Mossad also provided information about Iraq's secret nuclear plans, resulting in the 1981 Israeli Air Force bombing of the Osirik nuclear reactor in Iraq.

Members of Israeli Intelligence inspect
entrance to smuggling tunnel.

# CHAPTER 4
# Dana's Dilemma: The Army or Alternative Service

**Dana's family was religious,** and she attended a religious high school. About half of the girls in her class would join the army, while the other half would choose National Service (*Sherut Leumi*), which is an option for religious women. Dana knew her parents preferred that she choose alternative service but would leave the final choice up to her.

Dana appreciated the important work of National Service. She could work with sick children in a local hospital or tutor children from disadvantaged homes. She also knew that she would be able to dress more modestly in National Service. It would also be easier to observe the Sabbath and holidays.

On the other hand, Dana's family had emigrated from the United States when she was three. Her parents hadn't served in the army. Dana thought it was important to be a soldier in Israel, and she wanted to be the first in her family to serve in uniform. She hoped she could get an assignment that would allow her to do something important without compromising her religious observance.

Dana wasn't a star athlete, but she was active in the religious scouts and twice a week led a group of fourth graders in after-school activities. She spent her spare time reading, and her favorite school subject was Bible.

After she underwent all the army tests, she received a letter offering her about 30 different choices of jobs in the military. She could sign up for one of the new combat units that included women, be a secretary at army headquarters in Tel Aviv, or teach in an outlying community. She could organize classes for soldiers in army bases or teach Hebrew to immigrant soldiers. She was asked to indicate her first and second choices.

Dana decided to see where she would be assigned before making her final decision about whether to go into the army or into alternative service.

Women soldiers munch sufganiyot (jelly donuts) on Hanukkah.

Israel is the only country where military service
is compulsory for women.

## WOMEN IN THE IDF

Women serve in the armies of many countries, but Israel is the only country where military service is compulsory for them. They are drafted at the age of 18 and serve for at least two years. They go through two and a half weeks of basic training, which includes instruction in first aid and the use of weapons. Married women are exempt from serving, and religious women can choose alternative service, *Sherut Leumi*.

Although women soldiers had played a role equal to men in the Haganah, after the creation of the State of Israel, their participation was greatly reduced. In 1948 a special women's branch was created, first called the Auxiliary Corps and later changed to the Women's Corps. Women soldiers were assigned jobs as drivers, clerks, and support workers, but they could not fight.

Gradually, women were accepted into combat support roles as minesweepers, parachute packers, radar interpreters, and instructors for sharpshooters. In recent years, the rule barring women from applying for flight school was challenged in Israel's Supreme Court. In 1995 the rule was changed, and in 2001, Lieutenant Roni Zuckerman became the first woman to reach the status of fighter pilot. Other army positions are opening to women as the army strives for gender equality. Now women serve as combat soldiers, in the border police, and in one infantry battalion, the *Caracal*. In 2004 the Women's Corps was disbanded as a separate division of the army.

On Tu B'Shevat, members of the Navy join children in a hospital oncology ward to plant trees.

## WOMEN IN NATIONAL SERVICE

Young women, particularly those who are religiously observant, may choose other jobs under *Sherut Leumi*, the alternative service option. They can work in hospitals, teach children in disadvantaged areas, serve as nature guides, or help with immigrants. Young women in National Service don't wear uniforms and don't undergo basic training.

# CHAPTER 5
# Sharona Opts for a Fighting Unit

**Sharona spent a lot of time** thinking about what she wanted to do in the army. She was a good athlete and had studied ballet and jazz since she was little.

She thought she'd have a good chance of being accepted into the pilot's course, now open to women, but she knew she didn't want to spend the required seven years in the army. Ultimately, she wanted to be a doctor, and that would require many years of study after she finished her military service.

Sharona knew she didn't want a desk job. Her sister Miri had served as executive secretary to a high officer, but Sharona wanted more active service. Today there were more options for women than when Miri served. Sharona could become a fighter in a combat unit or she could aim for a pre-combat job, training men to handle tanks or weapons. She could also become part of the Military Police, responsible for enforcing army discipline and dress code, guarding military prisons, and monitoring border checkpoints.

Sharona was glad when a woman officer came to her high school to talk about the army. The officer was in charge of a squadron of women in a border police combat unit. This was the first time Sharona had met a woman who was an actual fighter. Sharona wondered if she'd be brave enough and strong enough to carry a submachine gun and to confront terrorists. She'd never been in a physical fight with anyone. After the lecture, Sharona had a chance to talk to the woman officer. She realized that the officer wasn't any bigger or stronger than she was. "I can do this," Sharona thought to herself.

Today there are many combat options for women in the IDF.

The IDF trains dogs to assist in search and rescue operations, identify explosives, and prevent border infiltration.

## GROUND FORCES

The largest section of the IDF includes the infantry (ground soldiers). When the IDF was created, it kept the names of the fighting units of the Haganah: the *Givati*, *Golani*, and *Nahal* Brigades. In addition. there are paratroopers and special forces (*sayerot*) that undertake reconnaissance and anti-terror missions. Soldiers with particular physical fitness, talent for navigation and map reading, independent thinking, and military intuition are recruited for these units.

## NAHAL

NaHaL is the Hebrew acronym for *Noar Halutzi Lohem* (Fighting Pioneer Youth), a military cadre unique to Israel. It originally combined combat service with civilian work in agricultural settlements. Nahal soldiers must be willing to put up with primitive living conditions for months at a time. Since 1948 Nahal units have established more than 100 new kibbutzim and settlements, many of them built to protect sensitive border areas. Today more emphasis is being placed on the combat aspect of Nahal service.

# PARATROOPERS

Israel's paratroopers are known for their daring and their strong fighting spirit. One of their legendary successes was during the 1956 Sinai Campaign with Egypt, which was the last time that Israeli paratroopers actually jumped out of airplanes behind enemy lines. In 1967, during the Six-Day War, they successfully fought to regain the Old City of Jerusalem. The photo of a paratrooper at the Kotel (the Western Wall) became the symbol of the victory of this war.

Since 1956, no paratroopers have been required to drop from airplanes, but the "red berets" are still trained to jump and proudly wear a wing-shaped badge on their uniforms. Soldiers from other branches of the military also can earn their wings in a three-week course at the IDF's Parachute School. Many IDF chiefs of staff were officers in the paratroopers.

*Israel's paratroopers are known for their daring and strong fighting spirit.*

## GOLANI BRIGADE – THE EYES OF THE NORTH

The Golani Infantry Brigade is usually stationed to protect the north, but its soldiers also take on outside missions, especially during wartime. In the Six-Day War and the Yom Kippur War, they fought hard in the Golan mountains, and in 1982 they conquered the Beaufort Mountain in Lebanon, from which terrorists had been firing on Israel's North.

The IDF's Tank Corps is a popular choice for recruits.

## GIVATI BRIGADE

This unit, usually stationed in the south of the country, has played a major role in defending the many isolated settlements in the Negev Desert. In recent years, Givati soldiers played a central role in protecting Israel against terrorist attacks from Gaza.

## TANK CORPS

On the winding road up to Jerusalem, you can see armored vehicles used during the War of Independence. At first, the IDF didn't have tanks and had to use trucks and buses reinforced with iron plates in the middle. These armored vehicles were called sandwich trucks. During the War of Independence, Israel had only 16 tanks, none of them new. Later, the IDF was able to purchase and recondition secondhand tanks: Shermans, Centurions, M-48s, and others.

Ultimately, Israel's leaders decided to build a new tank that could move quickly over difficult terrain and supply firepower. The Israeli tank was called the *Merkava*, the Biblical word for chariot. Its engine was in front to better protect the crew, and ammunition was stored in the least-exposed area of the tank so that it wouldn't easily catch fire. A rear hatch provided a way of getting in and out of the tank. The first Merkavas were produced in 1979. Today the tank has been constantly improved, and is considered one of the best in the world. The IDF's Tank Corps is a popular choice for recruits.

## ARTILLERY CORPS

The Artillery Corps also began with very old equipment. Its most famous weapon was called the *Davidka*, a homemade mortar with limited firepower. Today the corps makes use of the most accurate and sophisticated high-tech equipment. It was the first combat section of the IDF to use women instructors to train fighting soldiers.

## ENGINEERING CORPS

"The hard we shall do today; the impossible we shall do tomorrow" is the motto of the Engineering Corps. In the IDF engineering corps, sappers—soldiers specially trained to handle explosives—are attached to tank divisions and infantry to help overcome obstacles and dismantle bombs. In 1973, while under fire, they managed to build bridges across the Suez Canal, enabling the IDF to surround part of the Egyptian army.

The Engineering Corps using mine detectors during a field exercise.

Even on active duty, religious soldiers pray and read Torah.

## THE HESDER PROGRAM

Most religious soldiers serve in regular army units, but about a fifth of
the graduates of national religious high schools enter the *Hesder*
program. Hesder (which means "arrangement") is a framework which
combines yeshiva study with shortened military service. A soldier in the
hesder program commits to five years. The first year is usually a year of
yeshiva study prior to being inducted into the IDF. Then the soldier
spends four more years, including a year and four months in the IDF in
training and active duty.

The first hesder yeshiva, *Kerem B'Yavneh*, was founded in the 1950s.
Following the Six Day War, the program expanded throughout the country.

Most hesder students are men, though there is a program for women, *Hadas*, which combines yeshiva study with service in the Army's education and intelligence corps.

Religious soldiers who serve in the regular IDF may spend a *mechina* (preparatory) year in yeshiva study combined with basic army training. Afterwards they serve the full three years in the army.

Service in the IDF affords immigrants, such as those from the Soviet Union and Ethiopia, the opportunity to learn about and adapt to their new country.

## CHAPTER 6
# Becoming a Soldier

**A**fter much deliberation, Dana decided to join the army instead of alternative service.

Because their birthdays were close, she and David would begin their military service on the same day. Their friends gave them a party with music and lots of food, including Dana's favorite olive pizza with extra cheese. They told stories from their childhood, and Hezzy gave Dana a funny photo he had made of her riding on a horse like the one his great-grandfather rode when he served in the *Shomer*. Sharona gave her a mug with a picture of the four of them.

Male soldiers are subject to "army" haircuts!

Dana hugged her friends and wiped away a tear. "I'll miss you guys."

"Don't worry," said Sharona. "We'll see you next Friday. New soldiers always get the first Shabbat off."

Dana could hardly sleep the night before her induction. Knowing she needed to report at 8 A.M., she kept waking up and looking at her alarm clock. About 100 teenagers were already waiting when her parents dropped her off at the Induction Center. She was happy to see David in the crowd.

Two buses rolled up to the sidewalk. An officer took out a clipboard with a list of names. David's was among the first to be called. He hurried to the bus. A lot of other names were called. When finally she heard her own name, Dana's heart jolted. She turned to her parents and saw they were crying. Then she looked at David's parents and they were crying too.

Everyone on the bus was quiet. They weren't used to seeing their parents cry. Dana swallowed hard to keep from crying herself. When the engine roared and they pulled

New soldiers are given kit bags with
their uniforms and shoes.

away, everyone started talking at once. David winked at her
and made a thumbs-up gesture. "Hey, we're in the army,
now," he said. She was excited, and she felt proud.

It took an hour to get to the *bakkum*, the military center
in Tel Aviv. Thousands of new soldiers were gathered.
Dana waited to be fingerprinted, inoculated against
hepatitis, and have blood drawn to record her DNA. There
were lots of forms to fill out. But most exciting was getting
her kit bag with her green army uniform and shoes. She
also got a metal tag with her name and her ID number. That
was a little scary, because she knew the tags were for
identification if she were to be captured or killed. It
reminded her that the army wasn't summer camp.

An hour later, when Dana ran into David at the vending machine, she hardly recognized him. His long red hair had been cut back almost to his scalp.

That night Dana slept in bunk beds in a barracks with seven other recruits. They shared a common bathroom. She had been to overnight camp so that part didn't seem strange. Basic training would start the following week. First, she would get to spend Shabbat with her family, and because she was in uniform, she could ride the bus home for free. Standing tall at the bus stop, she felt proud to be a member of the IDF.

## UNIFORMS

Soldiers in all the land forces, (infantry, tank corps, communications, artillery, intelligence, logistics) wear working uniforms of olive green trousers and long-sleeved green shirts. On dress occasions, the officers wear a lighter green shirt and darker green trousers. Unlike officers in other armies, Israel's officers never wear neckties. Land forces wear black or reddish-brown boots that go just above their ankles.

All of the soldiers wear wool berets: red for paratroopers, black for tank troops, turquoise for artillery, bright green for Nahal, brown for Golani, purple for Givati, dark green for Intelligence, silver-grey for engineers, and blue for the Israeli Military Police.

Navy and Air Force soldiers also wear green uniforms for daily work. Sailors wear khaki in the street, but their dress uniforms are white. Air Force officers wear light blue shirts and dark blue trousers.

## CHAPTER 7
# Basic Training

**Even though David wasn't going** to be a combat soldier, he would have to complete a month of basic training. Afterward, he'd go for specific training for intelligence work. His friends in the infantry and engineering corps had four months of basic training; the tank and artillery recruits, three months.

David slept in a tent with seven others. Each day included 16 hours of hard work. The hardest parts for him was getting up at 5 A.M. every day and being awakened for special maneuvers in the middle of the night. For the first time in his life, he fell asleep during a lecture.

The course included first aid, how to handle a gun, shoot an assault rifle, defend himself against conventional and non-conventional weapons, and lots of rules about being a soldier. He learned that if someone in his unit broke a rule, the whole unit would be punished. Although everything was taught in Hebrew, David felt as if he were studying a new language because there was so much military jargon to learn. Often people spoke in funny-sounding acronyms, shortcut speech using the first letter of each word.

Basic training includes living in tents.

# CHAPTER 8
# Swearing In

**Part of the process** of becoming a soldier is a ceremony of swearing allegiance. Soldiers who object to saying, "I swear" because of the religious prohibition on making oaths, are permitted to say, "I affirm." Some branches of the army hold ceremonies at the Kotel, the Western Wall; others are held at army bases.

Since Dana was the first person ever in her family to serve in the Israeli army, she was particularly excited about her swearing-in ceremony.

There isn't much formal marching in the Israeli army, so she and the other women soldiers had practiced for this occasion. In one hand, she held a submachine gun. In her other hand was a Bible. A military band was playing a popular Israeli song about the need to give of yourself. Dana recognized another song from her Bible study: words from the prophet Zechariah: "Not by might, nor by power, but by My Spirit . . ." She blinked back tears.

Dana looked up and saw her parents smiling. With them stood Hezzy, Sharona, and David! She wanted to run to them, but the sergeant major called them to attention. Instead, she stood up straight and pledged her loyalty.

Some branches of the army
hold induction ceremonies at the Kotel.

## CHAPTER 9
# A Reunion

**The following summer** Sharona and David
met for hamburgers at their favorite Jerusalem restaurant.
David's assignment in Military Intelligence allowed him
to come home every other weekend.

"Do you like what you're doing?" Sharona asked.

"It's interesting," David grinned. "Very interesting, in fact."

Sharona knew she couldn't ask anything else. What
David did was classified. "What have you heard from
Hezzy?" she asked instead.

"So far so good," David said. "The first part of the pilot's
course is a lot of classroom study, and he's really good at
physics. The hard part will be when he has to show he's
good at flying airplanes."

"I'm betting that he'll make it," said Sharona. "He's the

only one of us who got his driver's license the first time around."

David nodded. "And it's great about Dana. She found the army job that fits her perfectly. She's going to be stationed near Beersheva, teaching Judaism to soldiers from the former Soviet Union. Their mothers aren't Jewish, and they want to convert while they're in the army."

Sharona took a bite of her hamburger. "It's an important job, and she's a natural teacher. I saw her mother last week, and her parents have come to terms with her decision to serve in the army."

"What about you?" David asked Sharona.

A little younger than the others, she wouldn't begin her army service until December. "I have a surprise."

David looked up. "What kind of surprise?"

"You remember that I'd thought I wanted to be an instructor for sharpshooters in the infantry? I've changed my mind. I'm joining the Border Police as a combat soldier in a special patrol unit." As soon as she said it, she wondered if David would feel bad. Before his injury, he'd been so eager for Navy combat. But he seemed genuinely happy for her.

"That's amazing!" David said. "What made you decide?"

"I was worried about being tough enough for combat, so I took a karate course and saw that I could do it."

"I'm sure you can," David said. "Good luck!"

"The training base is near Jerusalem, and Dana and Hezzy are in the South," said Sharona. "I hear there's a terrific hamburger place in Beersheva."

"I'll join you if I can," said David, who couldn't disclose where he was stationed. "And I'll bring the ketchup."

# BIBLIOGRAPHY

Israel Defense Forces: A People's Army, Lt. Col. Louis Williams, Ministry of
    Defense Publishing, 1989

www1.idf.il/ Official Website of the IDF

http://www.isayeret.com/guides/overview.htm- Israel Special Forces official
    website

http://www.iaf.org.il Israel Air Force official website

http://www1.idf.il/Navy Israel Navy official website

http://www1.idf.il/aman Israel Intelligence Corps official website (Hebrew)

http://www.mahal2000.com/links/military.htm- Volunteers for IDF, many
    links

http://www.10million.org Site for soldiers Missing in Action

http://www.mod.gov.il Ministry of Defense website

http://www.givati.org.il/ Givati Infantry official website (Hebrew)

http://www.gal-ed.co.il/totchanim/ Artillery Corps official website (Hebrew)

http://www.shiryon.co.il/ Tank Corps official website (Hebrew)

http://www.mossad.gov.il Official website of the Mossad

http://shabak.gov.il/mod/ Official website of the Israeli Security Agency

http://www.sabranet.com/machal/english.html Volunteers for War of
    Independence

# ABOUT THE AUTHOR

Barbara Sofer is a prize-winning journalist and author whose popular column is featured in *The Jerusalem Post* weekend edition. She is Israel Director of Public Relations and Communications for Hadassah, the Women's Zionist Organization of America. Her book *Ilan Ramon: Israel's Space Hero*, (Kar-Ben) was named a Notable Children's Book by the Association of Jewish Libraries. *Shalom, Haver, Good-Bye, Friend*, a photo essay in memory of Israel's Prime Minister Yitzhak Rabin, (Kar-Ben) won the 1997 Sydney Taylor Award for the best Jewish children's book. Her adult novel *The Thirteenth Hour* (Dutton/Penguin) won critical acclaim. The mother of five, Barbara lives in Jerusalem with her husband, scientist/writer Gerald Schroeder.